Trendy But Healthy Tik Tok Recipes

Innovative Tik Tok Dishes That Are Healthy

BY

Jasper Whitethorne

Licensing Notes

Table of Contents

Introduction

Tik Tok has had a bad rap for creating some bizarre food ideas, which makes many people question if they should trust the recipes shared at all. While this may be true in some cases, some digging around reveals that not all recipes shared on Tik Tok are bad. In fact, some are super healthy and effective tricks to creating simple innovative meals that are healthy.

You don't need to cook up a whole pot of risotto with these recipes as they are pretty simple passes.

Scanning around for healthy Tik Tok recipes, we came across some fantastic options that would improve your meal collections. They are made with nutritious ingredients, which are tweakable to your preference.

These thirty recipes span across snacks, drinks, breakfast, lunch, and condiments to improve your servings.

Are you ready to check them out? Let's head right into them.

1. Salmon and Rice Bowl

This recipe is such a great way to enjoy leftover salmon and rice. Placing an ice cube on the rice while microwaving adds moisture to the rice, bringing it back to life. Meanwhile, salmon and rice are rich in nutrients including the toppings of avocados, sesame seeds, and kimchi.

Prep Time: 15 mins

Cook Time: 2 ½ mins

Serves: 1

Ingredients:

- 1 to 2 cooked salmon filets
- 1 ice cube
- 2 cups cooked rice

For toppings:

- Diced avocado
- Soy sauce to taste
- Sriracha to taste
- Kewpie mayonnaise to taste
- Kimchi to taste
- Roasted seaweed sheets for serving

Instructions:

In a bowl, flake up your salmon into small bits and add the rice on top.

Place an ice cube at the center of the rice and loosely cover the bowl with parchment paper to allow steam to escape.

Microwave for 2 to 2 ½ minutes.

Take out the bowl, remove the parchment, and any residual ice cube.

Mix the rice with salmon and add your toppings.

Serve with seaweed sheets.

2. Parmesan-Crusted Potatoes

These are truly a better way to crust your potatoes with cheese, so those Parmesan bites are better and tastier.

Prep Time: 15 mins

Cook Time: 20 to 30 mins

Serves: 4

Ingredients:

- Olive oil, for drizzling
- 1 to 2 cups grated Parmesan cheese
- 9 potatoes, cut in half lengthwise
- 1 tbsp chopped fresh thyme or 1 tsp dried thyme
- Balsamic glaze, optional

Instructions:

Preheat your oven to 350°F and line a baking sheet with parchment paper.

Next, drizzle olive oil across the parchment paper and spread the Parmesan cheese all over it. Sprinkle the thyme across the cheese.

Place the potatoes directly in line on the Parmesan cheese with the flat side on the cheese. Make sure the open side of each potato is covered with cheese.

Bake in the oven for 20 to 30 minutes or until the potatoes are cooked.

The potatoes should have a beautiful golden cheese crust around it and come off the sheet easily. Top with balsamic glaze if preferred before serving.

3. Whipped Coffee

This trend has somewhat taken over quite quickly - it is everywhere now. By simply, whipping coffee and topping it on milk, you create a fluffier, rich, and sweet take on coffee. It's so good.

Prep Time: 15 mins

Serves: 1

Ingredients:

- 2 tablespoons hot water
- 2 tablespoons instant coffee
- 2 tablespoons sweetener
- 1 cup milk to serve, optional
- Ice cubes for serving, optional

Instructions:

In a bowl, combine the hot water, sweetener, and instant coffee. Whip on medium speed until light and fluffy.

Add ice cubes to a glass, top with milk, and spoon the whipped coffee on top.

Serve.

4. Whipped Matcha

Just like whipped coffee, wouldn't you like to enjoy your green tea this way?

Prep Time: 15 mins

Cook Time: 1 min

Serves: 4+

Ingredients:

- 2 tablespoons aquafaba (chickpea liquid) or egg white
- 1 tablespoon cane or granulated sugar
- 1 teaspoon matcha powder, culinary grade
- 1 cup milk

Instructions:

Whip the aquafaba or egg white in a bowl until frothy and mostly stiff. Add the sugar and whip until stiff peaks form.

Sift in the matcha powder and whip until incorporated.

Add milk to a cup and spoon the whipped matcha on top. Serve.

5. Pancake Cereal

When you're not sure what makes up your store-bought cereal, you might want to consider making some healthy pancake cereal. These are light, soak up milk well, and are delicious.

Prep Time: 15 mins

Cook Time: 1 min

Serves: 4+

Ingredients:

- 1 cup dry baking mix
- ½ cup milk + extra for serving
- 1 egg

Instructions:

Whisk the three ingredients in a bowl until smooth.

Spoon or pour the batter into a condiment squeeze bottle.

Heat griddle over medium heat and squeeze dime size batter on the griddle with space between them. Cook until the bubbles pop. Flip the pancakes and cook the other side for 1 to 3 minutes.

Transfer them to a bowl and serve with milk and your other preferred toppings.

6. Baked Feta Pasta

This discovery is probably one of our favorites. How convenient and scrumptious does tomato and feta combine well with cooked pasta. It creates a creamier effect with feta, which we love so much.

Prep Time: 15 mins

Cook Time: 35 mins

Serves: 4+

Ingredients:

- ½ cup extra virgin olive oil
- 8 ounces block feta cheese
- 2 garlic cloves minced
- 2 pints cherry tomatoes
- ¼ teaspoon sea salt
- ¼ teaspoon black pepper
- 8 ounces pasta of choice
- ¼ cup packed chopped fresh basil + extra for garnish

Instructions:

Preheat the oven to 400°F.

Spread the cherry tomatoes in a baking dish. Drizzle with olive oil and season with salt and black pepper. Mix well and spread the tomatoes across the baking dish.

Place the feta cheese at the center and flip a couple of times to be coated with the olive oil and seasoning.

Bake in the oven for about 35 minutes or until the cherry tomatoes burst and feta cheese melts.

While they bake, quickly cook the pasta according to the package's instructions. Drain the pasta, reserving ½ cup of it in case you'll need it for mixing.

Add the basil and garlic to the ready feta and cherry tomatoes, and mix well.

Add the pasta and then toss to combine, adding pasta liquid when necessary.

Next, garnish with more basil and then serve.

7. Matcha Martini

Looking for a healthy touch for your martini? Try out this yummy matcha version. Considering that The Martini has evolved over the years, this might just be the new take for this era.

Prep Time: 15 mins

Serves: 4+

Ingredients:

- 2 to 3 ounces matcha, brewed and cooled
- ½ ounce white creme de cacao
- 1 ounce vodka
- ¼ ounce simple syrup
- Pinch of matcha powder, for garnish

Instructions:

Combine all the ingredients in a cocktail shaker. Cover and shake until cold.

Next, strain the drink into a cocktail glass and garnish with some matcha powder.

Serve.

8. Cheese-Wrapped Pickles

Some like this and some hate it but whatever the case with over 1.6 million likes on Tik Tok, there truly has to be something delicious about this "guilty-pleasure" snack.

Prep Time: 5 mins

Cook Time: 1 min

Serves: 4

Ingredients:

- 4 cheese slices of choice
- One large dill pickle, cut into quarters lengthwise
- Olive oil for drizzling
- Ranch dressing for serving

Instructions:

Heat a little oil in a non-stick skillet.

Place one cheese slice in it and let it melt until it is gooey in the center and crispy on the edges.

Place one dill spear at the center and wrap the cheese over it.

Remove the cheese-wrapped pickled with a spatula onto a paper towel-lined plate to drain excess grease and crisp up. Repeat making the remaining dill spears the same way.

Enjoy the pickles with ranch dressing.

9. Bacon-Wrapped Pickles

While at pickles, what an awesome way it is to pump up its flavor with some crunchy bacon. Enjoy this quick treat.

Prep Time: 20 mins

Cook Time: 1 min

Serves: 4+

Ingredients:

- 1 dill pickle spear, cut into quarters lengthwise
- 4 bacon slices
- Barbecue seasoning, optional

Instructions:

For the pizzelle:

Preheat your air fryer to 400°F.

Wrap each dill spear with one bacon slice from one end to the other. Tuck the ends within and season with barbecue seasoning if using.

Place the wrapped pickles in the air fryer for 15 minutes or until the bacon is golden and crispy.

Transfer to a paper towel-lined plate to drain excess grease and serve.

10. Bacon Twists

Do you love your bacon crunchy? There's a new way to get your bacon even crunchier. It is called Bacon Twists and is super simple to make. Here you go!

Prep Time: 15 mins

Cook Time: 1 min

Serves: 4+

Ingredients:

- 4 bacon strips

Instructions:

Preheat your oven to 350°F.

Twist each bacon strip in an upward motion until straightly twisted and not wrapped in.

Place the bacon in the oven and bake for 20 minutes. Flip them and bake for 20 more minutes.

Transfer them to a paper towel to drain grease before serving.

11. Adult Capri Sun

If you ever thought that your Capri Sun dreams were lost as an adult, then sorry, we aren't engaging in your pity party. This Tik Tok trend brought our Capri Sun dreams back to life and here is how to make it.

Prep Time: 15 mins

Cook Time: 1 min

Serves: 4+

Ingredients:

- A bag of frozen fruits, size of choice
- White or fruit-flavored wine to taste
- Seltzer to taste, optional

Instructions:

Open up the top side of the fruit bag and add the wine and seltzer. Mix.

Dip in a long straw and sip away!

12. Taco Pickles

Ready to add some fun to your pickles? Simply add taco seasoning to your jar of pickles and you have a well-flavored treat.

Prep Time: 15 mins

Chill Time: 24 hours

Serves: 4

Ingredients:

- 1 jar of pickles, size of choice
- Taco seasoning to taste

Instructions:

Open the jar and add the taco seasoning. Cover the jar and shake until the seasoning is well-dispersed.

Refrigerate for 24 hours and get ready to enjoy.

13. 3-Ingredient Alfredo Fettuccine

Are your hunger pangs screaming at you? Here's a quick, creamy, and delicious Alfredo Fettuccine to silence them.

Prep Time: 15 mins

Cook Time: 15 mins

Serves: 2

Ingredients:

- ¼ to ½ stick salted butter
- 8 oz fettuccine
- 1 to 1 ½ cups grated Parmigiano-Reggiano cheese

Instructions:

Cook your fettuccine according to the package's instructions.

When almost al dente, melt the butter in a skillet over medium heat.

Add the cooked fettuccine and some of its cooking liquid to your desired consistency. Stir well.

Add the cheese of your desired quantity and stir until melted.

Dish your fettuccine!

14. Pesto Eggs

Pesto Eggs have been making rounds in many cookbooks lately, why not? These aroma-rich toasts surely deserve everyone's liking of them. They aren't only healthy and yummy, but introduce a new way to enjoy toasts than the traditional styles.

Prep Time: 15 mins

Cook Time: 5 mins

Serves: 2

Ingredients:

- 2 tbsp pesto
- 2 medium eggs
- 1 avocado, thinly sliced
- 2 slices of sourdough
- 1 tbsp ricotta
- 1 tsp runny honey
- A pinch of red chili flakes

Instructions:

In a non-stick skillet over medium heat, add the pesto and cook until the pesto warms through, is shimmering, and you can see the oils slightly separated from the pesto.

Add your eggs, cover the skillet, and cook for 3 minutes.

Meanwhile, toast the bread and then spread ricotta cheese on one side of each. Top with the sliced avocado.

When the eggs are cooked to your liking, spoon them onto the toasts.

Drizzle with honey and season with red chili flakes. Serve.

15. Creamy Lemonade

This lemonade is creamy and refreshing, we aren't sure where it has been all this while. It is yummy and there's no way around bad mouthing it.

Prep Time: 5 mins

Serves: 1

Ingredients:

- 3 cups of ice
- 2 cups of whipped cream
- ½ cup condensed milk
- Lemon juice to your taste

Instructions:

Add all the ingredients to a blender and blend away.

Pour into a glass, stick in a straw, and enjoy.

16. Watermelon Pizza

Finding ways to improve how watermelon tastes is always a delight to us. This version uses cream cheese as a base and tops with other juicy fruits.

Prep Time: 10 mins

Serves: 4+

Ingredients:

- 4 ounces cream cheese, at room temperature
- ½ teaspoon vanilla extract
- 4 ounces frozen whipped topping, thawed
- 3 tablespoons confectioners' sugar
- 1 slice whole seedless watermelon, about 1 inch thick
- Assorted fresh fruits for topping
- Fresh mint leaves, optional

Instructions:

In a bowl, whip the cream cheese, vanilla, whipped topping, and confectioners' sugar until smooth.

Spread the cream on the watermelon and add your preferred chopped or small fruits.

Slice and enjoy.

17. Smoked Cream Cheese

As if cream cheese isn't yummy by itself, smoking it elevates its flavor. You can simply smoke it directly or spread on some seasonings before smoking it. It is an amazing compliment for crackers.

Prep Time: 5 mins

Cook Time: 2 to 3 hours

Serves: 4+

Ingredients:

- ½ cup butter, melted
- 3 large eggs, at room temperature, cracked into a bowl
- ¾ cup granulated sugar
- 1 tsp ground cinnamon
- 1 ½ cups all-purpose flour
- 2 tsp baking powder
- ⅛ tsp salt
- ½ cup mini chocolate chips
- Vegetable oil, for cooking
- Powdered sugar for dusting

Instructions:

Preheat your smoker to 200°F to 250°F.

Place your cheese on a generous sheet of aluminum foil and brush it with olive oil. Now, season it with your preferred spice to your taste.

Place the cheese (with foil) in the smoker and smoke for 2 to 3 hours until golden and crispy.

Remove it from the smoker and serve it with crackers.

18. 3-Ingredient White Claw Slushies

Summer, here we come! Tik Tok has been up on its game with many drink recipes and we think this is one of our preferred yet. It is simple, creative, cheap, and perfect for summer's heat. Even better, based on the type of fruit used, you get to create different colors of the same thing for some fun.

Prep Time: 5 mins

Serves: 1

Ingredients:

- 1 (330 ml) can White Claw seltzer
- Ice
- Fruits of choice, fresh or frozen

Instructions:

Add all the ingredients to a blender and blend until slushy.

Pour into a cocktail glass and serve.

19. Cowboy Butter

This cowboy butter gives all other compound butters a run for their money. It is a quick sauce that is ready just in time for your steak. To say it is mouthwatering is an understatement until you try it.

Prep Time: 15 mins

Cook Time: 1 min

Serves: 4+

Ingredients:

- 6 tablespoons butter
- Fresh lemon zest to taste
- ½ lemon, juiced
- 4 garlic cloves, minced
- 1 teaspoon paprika
- 1 tablespoon Dijon mustard
- ½ teaspoon cayenne
- 1 tablespoon chopped fresh chives
- 2 tablespoons chopped fresh parsley
- 1 teaspoon chopped fresh thyme
- 1 teaspoon chili flakes
- Salt and black pepper to taste

Instructions:

Melt the butter in a saucepan over medium heat.

Add the lemon zest, garlic, lemon juice, paprika, Dijon mustard, and cayenne. Whisk until smooth.

Add the chives, parsley, thyme, chili flakes, salt, and black pepper. Whisk until well-combined.

Allow to cool and serve with steak or other preferred dish.

20. Ranch Pickles

We've been talking about some interesting pickles in this cookbook and we can't ignore some really good options out there. This ranch version would knock you off your feet.

Prep Time: 15 mins

Chill Time: 24 hours

Serves: 4

Ingredients:

- 1 jar of pickles, size of choice
- A packet of ranch seasoning or to taste

Instructions:

Open the jar and add the ranch seasoning. Cover the jar and shake until the seasoning is well-dispersed.

Refrigerate for 24 hours and enjoy.

21. 3-Ingredient Ice Cream

Everyone likes ice cream, whether lactose-rich or not. But making ice cream can be tedious, which is why this 3-ingredient recipe makes life all the easier.

Prep Time: 15 mins

Cook Time: 1 min

Serves: 4+

Ingredients:

- A can of sweetened condensed milk, size of choice based on your taste preference
- About 2 cups of heavy cream
- Your preferred flavoring agent, for example vanilla

Instructions:

Add your ingredients to a blender and blend until smooth.

If using, add ups like chocolate chips, fold them in at this stage.

Pour the mixture into a container and freeze for a couple of hours until firm.

There you have it, ice cream!

22. Spicy Pickled Garlic

Not got kimchi? Improve some pickled garlic with spice and seasoning. No need to pickle your garlic in this case.

Prep Time: 15 mins

Serves: 4+

Ingredients:

- A jar of pickled garlic, size of choice
- Sriracha to taste
- 1 to 2 tsp of gochutgaru (Korean chili flakes) or to taste
- ½ tsp dried thyme

Instructions:

Strain the vinegar off the pickled garlic.

To the jar, add the remaining ingredients. Cover and shake until well-combined.

Open the jar and serve.

23. Vodka Butter

This is merely butter infused with vodka. It goes great on charcuterie boards, on toasts, as spread, and meats.

Prep Time: 5 mins

Serves: 4+

Ingredients:

- 2 sticks of butter, softened at room temperature
- 3 ounces vodka

Instructions:

Whiz the butter and vodka in a blender or food processor until smooth.

Spoon into a bowl and use. How easy was that?

24. Jell-O Candy Grapes

Frozen candy grapes are a great option for kids and adults alike. You'd want to have them on hand always for easy snacking. You can freeze them as they are or add flavors like Jell-O.

Prep Time: 15 mins

Serves: 4+

Ingredients:

- A bag of grapes, rinsed
- A pack of flavored powdered Jello, size to your preference

Instructions:

Add the grapes to a large zipper bag and add the powdered Jell-O.

Seal the bag and shake vigorously until the Jell-O is well-distributed.

Freeze until the grapes are firm.

25. Air Fryer Pizza Sticks

Craving pizza but not up for working a dough? These simple mozzarella rolls with a drizzle of pizza seasoning would satisfy the craving.

Prep Time: 15 mins

Cook Time: 10 min

Serves: 4+

Ingredients:

- 2 to 4 tortillas
- 4 to 8 mozzarella cheese sticks
- Cooking oil spray
- Pizza seasoning of choice for sprinkling

Instructions:

Preheat your air fryer to 300°F.

Lay out each tortilla and slice each in halves.

Roll each piece around a cheese stick and sprinkle with the pizza seasoning.

Mist with cooking spray and place in the air fryer. Air fry for 8 to 10 minutes or until golden and crispy.

Remove them onto a plate and enjoy.

Try out other seasonings and cheeses as you like.

26. Malibu Pineapples

Spark up a tropical party all by yourself at home with 2 ingredients - pineapples and Malibu rum.

Prep Time: 15 mins

Serves: 4+

Ingredients:

- 1 jar of pineapples chunks, jar size of your preference
- Malibu rum to fill jar

Instructions:

Drain the juice out of the pineapples, which you can reserve for another recipe.

Pour in the rum and cover the jar. Refrigerate for **not more** than 24 hours else the pineapples will change color.

Enjoy the pineapples as a snack.

27. Prosecco Vodka

This is such a great snack idea for using up leftover Prosecco. They are great for decorating brunch drinks too.

Prep Time: 15 mins

Cook Time: 1 min

Serves: 4+

Ingredients:

- 1 pound seedless green grapes, rinsed and well-drained
- 2 cups Prosecco
- 2 ounces vodka
- Granulated sugar for topping

Instructions:

Pat dry the grapes with a clean napkin and add them to a bowl.

Cover them with Prosecco and vodka. Cover the bowl with cling film and refrigerate for 24 hours. Drain the alcohol after.

To serve, toss the grapes in sugar and enjoy.

28. Miso Pasta

There's been a trend of drinking miso soup for breakfast to boost health. Maybe adding some of that miso to pasta would boost up your nutrient intake too. How about some umami flavor on pasta?

Prep Time: 15 mins

Cook Time: 1 min

Serves: 4+

Ingredients:

- 1 pound linguine, spaghetti or other long pasta
- 6 tablespoons butter
- 3 tablespoons miso paste
- 1 cup grated Parmesan cheese
- 1 cup reserved pasta water
- Furikake, seaweed snacks, nori, sesame seeds or red pepper flakes to garnish

Instructions:

Cook the pasta according to the package's instructions. Drain and reserve 1 cup of the pasta water stirring the pasta.

Melt the butter in a skillet over medium heat.

Stir in the miso with the pasta water until smooth. Add the Parmesan and mix until melted.

Stir in the pasta until well-coated with the sauce and add your garnishes.

Serve warm.

29. Apple Cider Mimosa

This mimosa is quite tangy but is a good way to extend your intake of ACV for a health boost.

Prep Time: 2 mins

Serves: 1

Ingredients:

- 1 part apple cider vinegar, chilled
- 1 part sparkling wine, chilled

Instructions:

Combine the apple cider vinegar and sparkling wine in a Champagne flute.

Enjoy!

30. Whipped Brown Butter

Brown butter develops a unique rich, nutty aroma after a longer melting time, which transfers all that flavor to anything it is used for. This might just be a better option of regular butter for your spreads.

Prep Time: 15 mins

Cook Time: 1 min

Serves: 4+

Ingredients:

- 1 block of unsalted butter
- Ice
- Flaky sea salt

Instructions:

Melt the butter in a skillet over medium heat until it is caramel brown but not burnt.

Transfer the skillet to the ice bath and let the butter cool.

Whip the butter to your desired consistency, seasoning with flaky sea salt.

Conclusion

How convincing were these Tik Tok recipes?

They surely are healthy takes and can be used in several different ways.

We hope you found some cool options that you'll be trying soon. Hopefully, they'll improve your cooking too.

Author's Afterthought

Thank you!

Experiencing the heavens is how I feel, and it's all because of you, my dear reader, for helping me reach this point. I crafted this book specifically for you, and it holds great significance to me that you discovered and embraced it. Amidst the numerous books with similar content, you chose this one. These Goosebumps are truly exhilarating.

There's one additional favor I'd like to ask of you. Others are searching for the perfect book to download and enjoy, and your thoughts might be the nudge they require. Moreover, I'm eager to learn your opinions on the book as well. Your feedback will be incredibly beneficial.

Once more, thank you.

Jasper Whitethorne

Made in the USA
Columbia, SC
12 December 2024

49106706R00039